Networking in the Security Industry

An A to Z Guide to Networking for Military Service Leavers

by Jordan Wylie

©Jordan Wylie, 2013

All rights reserved. No part of this book may be reproduced or transmitted in any form or by any means, electronic or mechanical, including photocopying, recording, or by any information storage and retrieval system, without written permission from the author, except for the inclusion of brief quotations in a review.

The author would like to mention the charity Combat Stress (Charity No. 206002). A UK registered charity, Combat Stress works with Veterans of the British Armed Forces, and members of the Reserve Forces, through effective treatment and support for mental health problems.

Connect further with Jordan Wylie on Facebook at the following link:
facebook.com/TheTrainingWing

All other enquiries (including bulk orders) to networkingbook@securityvacancieslist.com

CONTENTS

INTRODUCTION	6
A IS FOR ATTITUDE	8
B IS FOR BUSINESS CARDS	10
C IS FOR CONNECTING PEOPLE	13
D IS FOR DELIVERING	16
E IS FOR EVENTS	18
F IS FOR FOLLOWING UP	21
G IS FOR GRATITUDE	23
H IS FOR HELPING OTHERS	25
I IS FOR IMAGE	27
J IS FOR JORDAN WYLIE	29
K IS FOR KEEPING ABREAST	31
L IS FOR LISTENING	33
M IS FOR MOTIVATION	35
N IS FOR NEVER GIVING UP	37
O IS FOR OPPORTUNITIES	39
P IS FOR PRACTICALITIES	41
Q IS FOR QUALITY NOT QUANTITY	43
R IS FOR RESPECT	45
S IS FOR SOCIAL MEDIA	47

T IS FOR TIME	49
U IS FOR USING YOUR DATABASE	52
V IS FOR VISION	55
W IS FOR WEBSITE	57
X-FACTOR	59
Y IS FOR YOU	62
Z IS FOR ZEST	64
AUTHOR BIO AND CONTACT INFO	67

Introduction

Network – Network – and Network
Network, Network and Network is a phrase that many people often told me was the key to success when searching for new job opportunities or the answer on how to develop a network of contacts when trying to break into the private security industry.

I often asked myself, *"What exactly does that phrase mean and what did it entail?"* Was I supposed to join various social network sites such as Facebook or LinkedIn, or was I simply to order fancy business cards off the Internet and give them to every person I met?

What I discovered is that networking is about building and maintaining long lasting relationships. Moreover, it has the ability to open new doors and to assist in identifying new opportunities in the quest for happiness and success in your career or in business. Since leaving the military nearly five years ago, after nine years of service to Queen and country, I have come to believe that networking is the most powerful weapon in my personal armoury to achieve these goals.

I decided to write this pocket guide to help those who, like me, don't necessarily have extensive experience in the corporate world of business and may find the act of networking uncomfortable or intimidating. In truth, it's a fine art and one that must be practised at every opportunity in order to attain proficiency and success.

The following pages contain an 'A-Z' guide of helpful hints and top tips to assist you in *your* quest for new opportunities and business development through networking. I wish you the best of luck and remember – *Network, Network and Network!*

A is for Attitude

Having the right attitude is probably one of the single most important factors that will influence your ability to be successful in the private security industry. Simply put, a positive attitude attracts positive people. Additionally, it will contribute to building your self-confidence while highlighting to others your determination to succeed as a security professional.

It's important to always be aware of the attitude you're projecting to the outside world and how it can affect the opinions of others about you. This has never been more apparent when meeting someone for the first time. Remember that you only get one chance to make a good first impression!

If your attitude is anything less than positive, I suggest you adjust it quickly in order to succeed in the development of new relationships with your business contacts and to enhance your ability to discover new opportunities. Conversely, a negative attitude will breed negative results, for people usually avoid interacting with those who always see the glass as half empty.

You may have served for many years in the military where your rank gave you the authority to issue orders to others – without concern towards how people portrayed you as an individual. In the civilian world, you're going to find that things work quite differently.

Despite your military experience of which you remain proud, it might not matter to prospective employers from what unit you have come or the rank you have achieved. In fact, you might have to start at the bottom of the command chain again. While you may find this disheartening, it is your attitude that will carry you through to success. Don't allow this fact to affect your ability to interact with others who may now be your superiors, even though you may be older than them and you were previously more senior to them in your service life.

Remember: Attitude is everything! Dennis and Wendy Mannering say, *"Attitudes are contagious."* They go on to inquire if yours are worth catching.

B is for Business Cards

The business card is one of the smallest, yet most powerful, marketing tools you have at your disposal. Carrying them at all times is an absolute must. They are formatted to fit in your wallet or card holder with ease and come in all different types and textures that range from paper to plastic to aluminum.

Business cards are a simple and extremely effective method for giving and receiving direct contact details. They should be accessible at all times, for you never know when a golden business networking opportunity will arise. Remember that business is *not* always conducted in the board rooms of CEOs and senior executives but, rather, often informally in bars, restaurants and other social areas. Consequently, make sure you always have a supply of cards to distribute. If you regularly travel, keep some in a side pouch on your bag or in the car.

Utilising business cards is a reciprocal act. Thus, just as important as handing out business cards is collecting the cards of others. You never know when you may require assistance from third parties, so it's important to retain any information given to you. When completing your follow-up, this will allow you to personalise the relationship/short interaction you had.

One good method that many networkers use is to write down a fact about each person met. This could include the name of a favourite football team, birth place, where you met him or her or anything else that will assist you in reengaging or breaking the ice the next time you have an opportunity to interact. Of course, if you're going to write this type of information on a person's card as a reminder, it's improper etiquette to do this in front of him or her. In some cultures, this could even be viewed as very disrespectful, or it may portray you as a person who is very forgetful.

The bottom line is that you should never be afraid to ask new contacts for their details. Generally speaking, people like to talk about themselves, so provide an opportunity for them to do so! If they don't have a card available, feel free to use one of your own cards upon which to write the information.

Again, I strongly advise that you never leave home without your business cards.

Furthermore, when collecting information about your connections, remember what Peter Drucker said: *"The most important thing in communication is hearing what isn't said."*

C is for Connecting People

You may not recognise it yet, but you probably have quite a circle of connections that includes a solid network of experienced and established security professionals. The private security industry is a natural progression for many former service men and women. You will find many of your former colleagues are already fully established as security operators, operations managers, directors, and some may even be running their own companies.

Take some time to identify who is doing what and where they are located. Next, create a master list. You may want to touch base with these people, especially if it has been a long time since you last connected. Let them know what you're doing and your new location. In turn, they can add you to their list. Again, think reciprocity!

The creation of this list provides you with an easily accessible data base of contacts and human resources that you may offer to your prospective employers. Having a strong credible network makes you a valuable commodity, for you can easily contact others for operational support, equipment supply or, in many cases, an employment opportunity.

There is an old cliché that says *"It's not what you know, it's who you know."* Never has an expression been more apparent than on the security circuit. Connecting people through personal recommendations and leads is by far the most effective method for achieving your goals and objectives quickly.

When connecting with people or making referrals, honesty and integrity are of the utmost importance. Therefore, be careful not to make promises or guarantees that you cannot keep; this will only discredit you in the future. Furthermore, if you are going to *name drop*, make sure you've reconnected with the person of the name being dropped and that he/she respects you and would provide a good recommendation. If not, this could end up as a potentially embarrassing situation, which could also discredit you in the future.

Although there is much camaraderie between those who have served – *especially* with those who served in the same military unit as you – this will not necessarily translate into an automatic job referral. This is because there exists a huge difference between the skill set of a very good soldier who is effective on the battlefield with that of a professional security consultant.

Although you may be very willing to help your fellow networker, it's also very important to protect your own reputation. Therefore, think carefully before connecting people or giving recommendations. Often, security contracts are compromised, and sometimes lost around the world, because a so-called 'security professional' is found guilty of malpractice or misconduct. Consequently, always ask yourself if the person you're recommending will represent the security company to the highest of professional standards or if this is simply a person with whom you had some of the best times of your life – most likely in the pub or regimental bar.

Remember, you live and die by your recommendations! Moreover, Friedrich Nietzsche reminds you that *"Invisible threads are the strongest ties."*

D is for Delivering

Delivering upon your word is very important in the security industry, as well as in the rest of your life. Therefore, if you make a promise, make sure you're able to fulfill it. You will discover that people will quickly lose respect for you, if you continuously make false claims or give someone your word and fail to keep it.

Good networkers find opportunities on a regular basis due to the fact they are continually building and enhancing their professional contact database. As your professional network evolves and develops, there will come a time when you will be fortunate enough to be in a position where you encounter multiple opportunities.

Even as your business grows, one thing to always keep in mind is that, if you have given your word or signed a contract, you should do your upmost to meet the requirements whenever possible. If you start to let people down or fail to deliver upon your commitments, your reputation will grow very quickly. However, it will be for all the wrong reasons.

Honesty is an important personality trait of any networker – not only with other people but, more importantly, with yourself. Don't let your appetite or desire to succeed quickly govern your commitment schedule. Think carefully about your bandwidth and what you could reasonably accomplish on your own or with a team. This will assist you in deciding which jobs are the right fit for you and the ones in which you will be able to deliver upon all the tasks, requirements and expectations.

Ralph Waldo Emerson said, *"All promise outruns performance."* Therefore, aim to under promise and over deliver!

E is for Events

Security networking events are designed especially for security professionals to engage with each other, as well as to provide an opportunity to interact and expand the professional network of all those in attendance.

Events come in all shapes and sizes and can be a great resource for the inexperienced networker. Conversation is encouraged, and this provides a venue where people will naturally want to talk to you. This will allow them to learn more about what you do, the range of your experience, and if there exists a possibility of working together for mutual benefit.

You should embrace these occasions and attend as many events as possible. Due to the wide range of attendees, these events are perfect opportunities for you to access contacts with whom you normally would not get a chance to meet in your daily scope of operations. Events are usually littered with security professionals from all different sectors, including, Close Protection, Maritime Security, Remote Medicine and many more.

If you're going to attend an event, keep in mind that, unbeknownst to you, you may be critically reviewed by others. In fact, there will be many occasions when you may not know the name, background or position of the people with whom you're interfacing. Accordingly, approach a networking event almost like a job interview. Dress smart; be polite and professional; maintain a positive attitude; and don't forget your business cards.

To help you plan before attending a security networking event, think of it similar to a military operation.

1. Consider what you want to achieve from the event.

2. Think about whom you're going to target and what you can offer to them.

3. Also, consider what others can offer to you and how you may politely ask for it.

Feeling self-confident is key when attending events, and this may not be instinctive for you. In fact, you may be a person for whom networking feels unnatural. But like confidence, it's a skill that can be mastered. It's truly a fine art, for it's not about giving your best sales pitch to as many people as possible. Instead, it's about building new relationships and earning people's trust.

Vince Lombardi said, *"Winning is not everything, but wanting to win is."* Therefore, you need to be in it to win it!

F is for Following Up

If you are to network successfully within the security industry, following up on your leads is a fundamental requirement. After an initial meeting or learning about an individual's details, it's important to reengage and reconnect to cement the budding relationship. This is especially true with the security professionals you encounter after an event or, perhaps, a security conference or exhibition.

There is no right or wrong way to follow up on a lead; it all depends on the particular person and circumstances. Normally, a follow up would be carried out in the form of an e-mail, a phone call or it may even entail a pre-arranged meeting. Work towards striking the right balance between not allowing yourself to be forgotten by waiting too long to initiate contact and not wanting to appear desperate by inundating a person with calls, e-mails and the like.

Whichever way you chose to follow up, you must remember that this may be your last chance to build your credibility with the other person. Therefore, don't underestimate the time you need to spend in deciding upon your strategic approach to this all important technique.

Good networkers will reference distinctive topics from a previous discussion (the initial meeting) to start building a bond. It could include something about which your contact appeared passionate or about which he expressed strong opinions. It could also be as simple as mentioning something you both had in common, such as supporting the same sports team.

It's always a good idea to propose a next step, for example a meeting, a phone call, etc. In this way, you're offering the person the opportunity to take the relationship to the next level – to make a commitment to move forward together. Follow ups should not be underestimated and form an integral part of networking to success.

Anthony Robbins said, *"Success comes from taking the initiative and following up."* He challenges you with the following question: *"What simple action could you take today to produce a new momentum toward success in your life?"*

G is for Gratitude

Always remember to thank new contacts, business associates and clients for their time, business and support. It's important to show that you value them and are grateful for any contacts, referrals or assistance they may offer to you. Remember, good manners don't cost a thing, and *please* and *thank you* are two powerful words that will always serve you well.

Expressing your gratitude to others is a small building block in the quest to develop successful relationships with new people as well as deepen your bond with existing contacts.

There are many benefits to showing gratitude, and the effects it will have on all areas of your life are immeasurable. By taking simple steps to incorporate appreciative mannerisms and gestures in your day-to-day working environment, you will be able to generate support from the people with whom you interact in the security industry.

Be aware that if you fail to express your gratitude to those who help you, this will have a negative effect on your career because it will decrease the amount of assistance you will receive in the future. After all, everyone likes to feel appreciated and enjoys a sincere thank you!

Along with expressing your gratitude in your professional life, it's also very important to be grateful in your personal life. Gratitude nourishes your soul. When you're able to be grateful for what you have *vs.* bemoaning what you don't have, you are exhibiting faith in your current situation by believing that it's only going to get better. This naturally sparks feelings of positivity, which, in turn, others start to notice and to which they are drawn. And isn't that the point of networking ... to entice others to become part of your circle?

William A. Ward asks you a simple question: *"God gave a gift of 86,400 seconds today. Have you used one to say 'thank you'"?*

H is for Helping Others

Networking is as much (if not more) about helping others than it is about helping yourself.

Throughout your days in the military, much of the success you had in training, regimental life and more so on operations depended on team work and the ability to help others. This is a valuable trait that you should certainly carry through into your career within the private security sector.

It is often said that *what goes around comes around*. In business, people have long memories, and this can often be a double-edged sword for they will remember the good *and* the bad. Work hard to instill only good memories in the minds of your contacts.

Although you may be extremely busy in your day-to-day life, never overlook the importance of taking the time to make an introduction for someone. Although this shouldn't be your only reason for offering assistance, be assured that, if you do help a person, they will more than likely help you later on, if the occasion arises. It probably won't be your turn to benefit from your good deeds overnight. In fact, it may happen years later, in a roundabout fashion, or maybe never at all. Success from networking often comes when you least expect it.

Large networks of individuals can be very complex, and at times it's not possible to see exactly how or why they are working for you. It's imperative to believe and trust that your actions will be rewarded, even if the process is hidden or unclear in the moment and the effect takes a long time to materialise.

Consider following the wise words of William James, who instructs you to *"Act as if what you do makes a difference. It does."*

I is for Image

A trait that is often seriously misinterpreted is one's image.

Many of you may think your image relates to your physical presence – perhaps, how smart you look in your uniform or best suit or how tidy or stylish you keep your hair. This could not be any further from the truth! Image is not about what YOU think about anything. In fact, it's quite the opposite and concerns what other people think about you. Image is all about perception – how others feel about you and their evaluation of you as a person.

Each time you encounter a particular individual – perhaps at a networking event or at a security tasking – that person continues to build up a profile in his head based on his interactions with you. Very much in the same manner as a reputation, your image will always precede you.

There is a lot of talk between people in the private security sector. Due to this fact, people will have a perception of what and who you are based on informal passing comments of others within the industry.

The power of your image should never be underestimated – although you *do* have the power to control this by the way you conduct yourself (in person, by phone or email). If perchance you have generated a negative image, it's never too late to change this perception. However, I'll note that, if you're known to be a bad apple, the news will more than likely spread quickly and you'll have to work extra hard to remedy this situation. Of course, the best course of action is to never allow your image to become tainted or tarnished.

Perception can often turn into reality. Accordingly, keep in mind what, Deborah Tannen said: *"The key to conversation at work is flexibility and understanding how what you say might be perceived by others."*

J is for Jordan Wylie

Yes, that's right – it's me! I thought I would use this opportunity to expand my network, hopefully, to a worldwide audience. I know this may be slightly optimistic on my part; however, as I tell you in this book: take advantage of every opportunity which presents itself to you. So, I'm just following my own advice!

After finishing my military career in the British Army, I've been fortunate to find work in many security based roles that have ranged from protecting commercial shipping vessels from pirate attacks to providing close protection for high profile sports stars. So far, my journey has certainly been interesting and challenging, as well as very rewarding to say the least.

After leaving school with no academic qualifications, I recently obtained my degree (BA Hons) in Security and Risk Management. Personally, this was a great achievement and has opened up many other avenues to me as a security consultant.

Education and CPD (Continued Professional Development) goes hand-in-hand with networking, in my opinion. Although networking can help you to find opportunities through your contacts, ultimately, it's imperative that you have the knowledge and competency to deliver upon your security assignments. There is an old saying that says, *You're only as good as your last job*. This is extremely true when it comes to working in the private security sector.

Although, at times, the security industry can be very dangerous – very much like the military – it offers a very rewarding career for those who are willing to work hard. However, unlike the military, it can also be unforgiving and a small mistake could literally cost you your job or your employer their contract.

At present, I am employed as a Director of Operations within a security training organisation and have been fortunate enough to be involved in various training projects with military, police and government forces from all four corners of the world. I hope to be able to help others build their future careers through training, development and by providing advice from the lessons I have learned to date.

K is for Keeping Abreast

To remain current in the private security sector, it's necessary to keep abreast of any industry developments that may have a direct or indirect impact on you or your network.

Keeping current with legislative and regulatory changes enables you to become a good source of information for others to utilise. In turn, you will find yourself slowly becoming the 'go to' man or woman for networks close to home such as colleagues, associates and friends within the industry. Expanding your scope of knowledge can also provide you with a great platform, in case you desire to progress to higher networking circles and, perhaps one day, become a key influencer of industry changes.

To be a smart security networker, you have to stay tuned in to the field in which you wish to excel. There are many ways you can keep abreast, some of which include the following.

1. Attending conferences and events

2. Reading online blogs

3. Subscribing to industry news letters

4. Contributing to social media forums

Furthermore, in an ideal world, you will continue to be drip fed up-to-date information from a variety of sources, which often includes the people within your network.

If you can keep abreast of current issues, you will also be able to contribute more effectively when establishing relationships by conversing with strangers or other security professionals.

Peter Drucker said, *"We now accept the fact that learning is a lifelong process of keeping abreast of change. And the most pressing task is to teach people how to learn."*

L is for Listening

Listening to other security professionals will not only help you to learn about the industry, it will, more importantly from a networking perspective, allow you to evaluate them and what they have to offer in terms of experience, skill set and contacts. In general, if you're able to understand what a person needs, this helps you to figure out how you can help them develop their own opportunities.

Listening is a networking skill that is often overlooked and undervalued. Many, especially former soldiers, have a habit of being on 'permanent send' when they are conversing and don't provide an opportunity for others to meaningfully interact. Adopting the 'permanent send' approach has the tendency to highlight you as a hard salesman/woman who only engages in conversation to deliver a very direct pitch. This approach will quickly have a negative effect on those around you and usually fails to produce effective results in networking circles.

My advice is to always be polite, professional and listen to other security networkers pitch their business or services before you talk about what you have to offer. This allows you to listen, digest and understand how you could help them.

Offering a helping hand *first* usually makes a person more receptive to what you have to say next. Furthermore, although it can be tempting to keep one eye wandering around the room for other opportunities – especially ones you may deem more exciting or worthwhile – make sure to focus your attention solely on the person in front of you. Direct eye contact makes all the difference in establishing a rapport. Any behavior other than this can appear rude, negating any opportunity that may have been available to you. Treat each person as a valuable resource, for you never know what priceless assistance he or she might offer to you.

G. K. Chesterton said, *"There's a lot of difference between listening and hearing."*

M is for Motivation

If you've come from a service background, you are sure to understand why motivation is so important to achieving objectives or goals.

Opportunities in the world of networking are often missed due to a lack of motivation. There may be plenty of chances for networking, such as attending an event or seminar, but when the given time arrives, you may not feel motivated to attend or regard it as a bother to get up and go to it. This is a lackadaisical approach to building a business, and it will be reflected in your lack of success in your endeavors.

With some reflective thought, you will be able to determine the types of things or circumstances that stir your motivation. You may want to consider the idea that at the root of a lack of motivation there could be a fear of failure OR a fear of success. While you might understand your actions due to a fear of failure, it's often not so easy to ascertain those due to a fear of success, which often causes you to self-sabotage. Both failure and success are scary experiences because each situation brings change into your life, something to which most have difficulty adjusting – even if the end result might bring you to a better place. It's important to keep in mind that success doesn't arrive in one fell swoop. It occurs in increments, which gives you plenty of time to adapt to the changes it brings to your life.

Most highly motivated people harbor a strong desire to achieve success. This propels them to explore every opportunity available, no matter the size or distance. Socialising and networking with similar minded people is infectious. It may also become competitive, for there are many vying for the same positions. However, remember that competition is always healthy and pushes you to strive to do your best.

Raymond Chandler said, *"Ability is what you're capable of doing. Motivation determines what you do. Attitude determines how well you do it."*

N is for Never Giving Up

At times, it can feel like you are attending an endless amount of events, training courses or even interviews. Despite all this activity, you may still find yourself up against a brick wall and not having much luck connecting with the right people. When this happens, it's easy to start feeling as if you are wasting your time trying to build your profile in the security industry.

Please know that we have ALL been there. I understand and appreciate that it's not easy to pick yourself up or remain positive while in the midst of these types of situations ... but you must! Jesse Jackson advises, *"If you fall behind, run faster. Never give up, never surrender, and rise up against the odds."*

You will undoubtedly hear negative comments about people or companies. In fact, you may even read them online in social media groups or industry forums. However, your circumstances can change in an instant, for you never know when a small moment, which you may regard as innocuous, can make a tremendous difference. Accordingly, it is very important to remain positive, for success from networking normally comes from whom and when you least expect it.

Harriet Beecher Stowe said, *"When you get into a tight place and everything goes against you, till it seems as though you could not hang on a minute longer – never give up then, for that is just the place and time that the tide will turn."*

O is for Opportunities

There are opportunities to network all around you, although you may not always recognise them, or, if you do, you may not have the confidence to take advantage of a particular situation. In fact, opportunities are often missed because you're too busy broadcasting about yourself *vs.* tuning into what others are saying and sharing. Orison Swett Marden wrote, *"Opportunities? They are all around us. There is power lying latent everywhere waiting for the observant eye to discover it."*

Networking and taking advantage of opportunities does not have to be as complicated as you may imagine. It's simply important to keep an open mind, which includes not ruling out connecting with people just because they aren't directly associated with the business of security. Much like any other organisation or industry, all security operations need support from other areas, such as administration, human resources, logistics, finances, legalities and so on.

Think about how you met the people with whom you choose to socialise with today.

At some point, you would have had an initial interaction or encounter with them. Perhaps this occurred due to a shared common interest of some sort, which could include, overlapping business interests, similar familial backgrounds, shared enthusiasm for a sport, or a similar military experience. Naturally, you would exchange phone numbers and e-mail addresses. This gives you the perfect opening to stay in touch and further your relationship to turn it into a true friendship.

This is networking in its simplest form. You can apply these same principles to business networking.

P is for Practicalities

Be practical at all times. After all, there are only so many hours in a day and you need to eat and sleep, if you are going to be a good and effective networker.

One of the practical matters of business is planning. Paul J. Meyer said, *"Productivity is never an accident. It is always the result of a commitment to excellence, intelligent planning and focused effort."*

Taking that advice to heart, plan each day in advance. Ask yourself, *"What exactly do I want to accomplish today?"* It's very easy to get sidetracked from your plan, especially with the attractive distractions of social media and the Internet. Although these are both great tools for connecting with people, your consumption needs to be harnessed so you utilise them properly and to your best advantage.

Furthermore, plan your weekly, monthly and yearly calendar, too, if possible. For example, if you're going to attend security conferences, exhibitions, trade shows or industry networking events then you will need to budget the funds to do so. Often there is an entry fee, or you may need to travel or find accommodations.

Former U.S. President Dwight D. Eisenhower said: *"Plans are nothing; planning is everything."*

Q is for Quality NOT Quantity

When it comes to building a networking circle, bigger is *not* necessarily better.

Although networking is about building a database of contacts that allows you to expand and develop your personal network, attention to detail should be given to those with whom you choose to network.

Networking is certainly not a popularity contest, and it shouldn't be treated as such. Attending events that hold no value or adding LinkedIn contacts without relevance to your business will only consume precious time. Eventually, this becomes burdensome busy work that keeps you too occupied to pursue viable leads.

Going to one networking event with spot on people is much more beneficial than attending an event each night for people mostly outside of your target audience.

Here's a bit of advice from Emile Zola that you should <u>avoid</u>: *"If I cannot overwhelm with my quality, I will overwhelm with my quantity."*

R is for Respect

There are two main types of respect: self-respect and respect for others, and they are inextricably tied together. I'm sure that you have or should have mastered both in your military service days.

Respect forms the basis of all good relationships in life, and the networking domain is certainly no different. It's important to master self-respect first. You must ask yourself: *How can I expect others to show me respect, when I don't exhibit respect towards myself?* Furthermore, Mark Twain wants you to consider the fact that *"when people do not respect us we are sharply offended; yet in his private heart no man much respects himself."*

When networking, you should always consider how your comments or actions will be received by others. For example, *Will your comments offend people? Is there a possibility your opinions could be misinterpreted?*

Furthermore, think about the way you answer the phone or the type of words and grammatical syntax you employ in your responses to e-mail queries. E-mail can be especially tricky because, unless the recipient knows you well (and perhaps your brand of humor), innocent comments can be blown out of proportion. To be on the safe side, operate on the premise that that if something can be taken the wrong way, it will.

Additionally, consider the company you keep or take along to security networking events. You may often be judged on the actions of your associates, friends or colleagues. Consequently, if they are known to be disrespectful or ill-mannered, you may be unfairly tarred with the same brush.

My best advice is to attempt to treat and speak to others as you would expect them to do to you. And, as Clint Eastwood said: *"Respect your efforts, respect yourself. Self-respect leads to self-discipline. When you have both firmly under your belt, that's real power."*

S is for Social Media

Social media is a powerful tool for networking, which simply put is the cultivation of productive relationships for employment or business. It's a mutual sharing where both parties should be able to reap benefits. Simon Mainwaring explains it as follows: *"There is a fundamental shift that social media necessitates in business today – the need to transition from 'Me First' to 'We First' thinking."*

LinkedIn, Facebook and Twitter are excellent sites for building contacts and developing relationships. To use these tools effectively and to reap the most benefit, when you reach out to someone through these venues, avoid sending the canned message that is automatically generated. For example, on LinkedIn, rather than clicking on someone's profile and simply asking him/her to be added to your network, personalise your message with information that is potentially helpful to your prospective connection. If you're contacting someone with whom you've had no prior contact, they are more apt to respond in a positive manner with this sort of advantageous (to them) message.

Social media sites are also very useful to discover *who's who* in your specialist sector. However, be forewarned that there is a downside to posting online. These sites are also used by many security employers to monitor their staff in order to see what they are doing in their spare time and to make sure that they are conducting themselves properly at all times.

Of course, if you work in the security industry, managing your social media security settings so that only the people who you want to see your posts should be easily handled.

When accessing these sites, keep in mind the words of Margaret Atwood: *"Social media is called social media for a reason. It lends itself to sharing rather than horn-tooting."*

T is for Time

Time will always be your greatest resource. With the busy schedule of an entrepreneur or an independent security consultant, it will often seem like there are not enough hours in the day.

While it may seem inconceivable for you to save an hour a day, the secret to achieving this objective is to try to save minutes on each of your tasks. If you can do that, before you know it, an extra hour will be yours. Follow the prescription set forth by Golda Meir, who said: *"I must govern the clock, not be governed by it."*

Before you start on any time management scheme, you must decide upon your priorities. Keep in mind that perfectionism and time management are not necessarily compatible. The first step is to make a list of all your responsibilities, activities and commitments. Upon examining this list, decide which can be eliminated, modified, shared or reduced.

Here are 9 time saving hints.

1. Learn to say no, nicely of course. It's not necessary to attend every networking event to which you're invited.

2. When completing follow-ups, limit interruptions by turning on the answering machine on a landline and only checking your voice mail on a mobile phone at predetermined times throughout the day. Additionally, learn to firmly end conversations, meetings, etc.

3. Use a calendar to avoid overbooking or double booking commitments.

4. Learn to delegate when possible.

5. Spend time on instituting a comprehensive filing system so that every piece of paper has its place and is always within reach. If you store your files electronically, take the time to organise your desktop into folders that segregate different areas of information. Keep track of the business cards that you collect during networking events. *(See the next section "U is for Using Your Database" for further detail on this subject.)*

6. Manage other's expectations by asking: *"What do I want?" "What do they want?"* and *"Can I do it?"*

7. Make a daily to do list; prioritise items and then constantly revise it as circumstances change.

8. Don't procrastinate; do your worst task first and get it over with.

9. Make sure to schedule personal time. This will refresh and rejuvenate you so that, when you return to work, you're able to refocus on your tasks.

Obviously, this is a very simplified list, and each person must individualise a time management plan that fits his/her own lifestyle, job and family. The most important thing seems to be the ability to let go of the little things. Although you always want to be precise, striving for perfection can hamper your ability to complete any of your tasks.

U is for Using Your Database

As you continue to build your network, you will make a habit of collecting business cards and contact details. Once they are in hand, you need to ensure you stay on top of your personal administrative duties. For example, don't just leave the cards sitting in a pile on your desk or stuffed into your wallet. Instead, create a simple database using a programme such as Excel.

Choose, with careful and thoughtful analysis, the people who you feel would best fit into your database. Select viable candidates by focusing on quality *vs. quantity*. This ensures the construction of a more effective networking database.

A database can be started by entering contact information and any other relevant details under the following headings, although feel free to add any other ones that you find applicable.

1. Name
2. Business Name
3. Website URL

4. Mobile Number

5. Office Number

6. E-Mail Address

7. Physical Address

8. Contact Date (when and where)

9. Follow-up Date

10. Outcome(s) from each interaction

11. Miscellaneous (perhaps an interesting fact or an interest you hold in common with the person)

Additionally, if you have a task to complete that assists one of the people in your network, you can add this information (and the date due) into your database to ensure a timely delivery of your work. Also, make sure to add this to your calendar and set a reminder, at least a few days to a week before it's due.

It's prudent business protocol to avoid using your network *only* when you want something. Remember, networking is as much about giving than it is about receiving.

This simple database is a valuable commodity. When used properly, it can play a pivotal role in expanding your personal database of contacts, as well as being instrumental in generating increased revenue for your own business.

For example, if you produce a newsletter that is distributed by e-mail to clients, customers or security associates, use your database entries and insert the names into an auto sender program. This will help you to be more efficient with your time.

In order to generate more leads (and subsequently more revenue), each newsletter, in addition to providing timely and informative articles, should also include a *Call To Action*. This tells the readers of the newsletter what you would like them to do, which could include: visit your website, like your Facebook page, connect via LinkedIn, attend an upcoming networking event, review a book or magazine article you have written, take advantage of a special you are offering, or set up a free 30-minute consultation.

V is for Vision

For better success, it's important to develop a well-thought out *Action Plan*. If you can't envision where you want to go or what you want to achieve from networking then it will be very difficult for you to realise your goals. In fact, Helen Keller said, *"The only thing worse than being blind is having sight but no vision."*

Think about the time you spent in the military. You may have wanted to get promoted, gain experience on operational tours or go adventure training. Now that you're starting on a new career path in the security industry, you must decide upon the new things you want to accomplish.

To help you construct an Action Plan, the following are some beginning things about which to think:

1. Make a list of your top three priorities upon which you intend to focus.

2. Decide how you will hold yourself accountable.

3. Decide who you can ask to support you in these endeavors.

4. Decide how you will measure your success.

As you build your new career, you may face both similar and different challenges to the ones you encountered in your service life. Furthermore, the obstacles *you* see may be ones of which only you're aware, just as other things may be easier for you than others. Defining, and then honing, a clear vision of what you want to achieve will help you to overcome hurdles, as well as assist you in playing to your strengths.

Jonathan Swift said, *"Vision is the art of seeing what is invisible to others."*

W is for Website

Having your own website may seem a little over the top, especially if you've just left the military and have very little experience in the private sector as of yet. Don't be deterred by this situation.

Many security professionals have their own website, for there are a myriad of benefits to be reaped from it. One such benefit is that it allows you to instantly bridge geographical network barriers. With the flick of a mouse, people from the other side of the world can easily see what you do and from where you can do it. In turn, this allows you to potentially build your contacts without the need for an initial face- to-face interaction.

Having a website also offers people the flexibility of convenience. As previously discussed, time is often your greatest resource. Using it wisely, and providing a venue for others to be efficient as well, is often the key to success. For example, if someone can simply open his laptop and get an informative insight into who you are and what you have to offer, they may be more likely to feel comfortable contacting you in the future, if your services appeal to them.

A website will also improve your level of credibility, both as a small company and as an individual. Today, most people use the Internet to research people and companies to assist them in making strategic and calculated decisions relating to business, including the contracting of security services. Often, if a person cannot be Googled, a potential client may feel there are too many unknowns to pursue further contact. When choosing between a known commodity *vs.* an unknown one, familiarity (or, at least, having some information available) usually wins.

Before constructing your own website, peruse the websites of others in the same industry. There's no reason to reinvent the wheel, although you should not copy another company's site. However, you may want to include similar *categories* of information. Do make sure to link your website to your own social media feeds and also highlight your direct contact e-mail address to provide a platform for immediate communication in case someone wishes to engage with you further.

X-Factor

Every individual has an *X-Factor*. It's imperative for you to discover yours, which will allow you to play to your strengths.

An *X Factor* is what makes you distinctive and interesting to others. Perhaps your X-Factor is made up of the combination of your experience, qualifications or a skill set that is unique to you.

Take the appropriate time to determine what distinguishes you from the rest of the pack. Once you unearth your distinctive powers, you can use these features as a foundation upon which to build. Moreover, ascertain what you can do to remain memorable in the minds of your prospective contacts and clients when you're no longer in front of them. Joel Osteen, author of *Your Best Life Now: 7 Steps To Living at Your Full Potential*, suggests: *"Be the one to stand out in the crowd."*

Here are five suggestions on how to prepare for exhibiting your X-Factor during networking opportunities.

1. Before any event, complete research on the companies and/or people who you know will be in attendance. When you approach individuals, offer an interesting bit of trivia of which they may not be aware as it relates to their business.

2. Foreshadow the type of customer service you will provide by following up immediately after your first contact.

3. Offer a free product or service that works so well that it will entice them into pursuing you for more information.

4. Keep notes on personal tidbits about prospective clients, for example, their likes and dislikes; children's names; pet's names, etc. By letting them know that they were memorable to you, you will become memorable to them. Remember, what goes around, comes around!

5. After an event and when completing your follow-up calls, befriend and show your appreciation to the secretary, receptionist, or the assistant of the person with whom you want to connect. These are the people who can

hold the key to obtaining the appointments you desire.

Y is for You

You are no longer on the battlefield nor do you need to be on parade each morning. Your new life as a security professional is going to require you to undertake quite an adjustment. Don't minimise the amount of time that it will take to transition from a life of service to that of a private citizen. There are new routines to be learned and proper civilian protocol to fully digest and incorporate into your everyday life.

You may feel uncomfortable for a while until this new of way of living becomes more natural. However, you can also look upon this time as a reset for you or as a *"do-over."* So, although it may be unnerving to be without the camaraderie of your military unit or the security of job safety, it can also be a very exciting time in your life. Now, you're able to build a new life. You can construct it in the fashion that most suits you as the experienced and wiser adult you are now *vs.* the young and, perhaps, naïve boy or girl who embarked upon a military career many years ago.

Of utmost importance is to work on honing your people skills. Remember, not every situation is about you! It's often necessary to let go of your ego and a desire to always be right. One way to accomplish this feat is to avoid taking every comment you hear personally. C.S. Lewis wrote: *"Humility is not thinking less of yourself, it's thinking of yourself less."*

The security sector is very much client driven, which means you will often interact, engage and network with your own clients or those of your employer's on a daily basis. These individuals may well be senior business executives, celebrities or royalty. Here's where your people skills come into play. Become aware of how you present yourself. Listen carefully to the language you use. Be cognisant of how you conduct yourself at all times. In essence, you must self-monitor yourself to ensure you're always presenting the best version of yourself. If you're successful, this will have an immediate impact on all aspects of your role as a security professional.

Z is for Zest

The initial stages of transitioning from military to civilian life may be fraught with difficulty. So much so, you may want to give up. When you are experiencing dark moments of doubt, it may seem as if you have lost your fire, or the light in your life has been turned off. That is *not* the case; it continues to burn on a low flame as it waits for you to make the appropriate adjustments and learn how to adapt to the changes around you.

During difficult periods, it may be a good idea to withdraw for a short time to improvise, adapt and overcome as you did in the military. However, it's equally important to keep yourself tethered to life and the people who continuously support you through the highs and lows that life brings, such as your family and friends.

So, if you're discouraged because your networking forays are not bringing you the success you imagined you would find on the timetable for which you hoped, attempt to reignite your zest and appetite for being a person who can get the job done. Your service days have taught you a lot, and you have certainly overcome much tougher obstacles and challenges than those with which you are now being faced.

Adding zest back into your life starts with you. Find something about which to be proud and joyful, and you will be presented with more situations in which you will be able to find joy and feel proud about your accomplishments. Norman Vincent Peale said, *"If you have zest and enthusiasm, you attract zest and enthusiasm. Life does give back in kind."*

In truth, life is messy and can be an ostensibly endless list of tasks and responsibilities. At times, it may even seem as if you spend all your time jumping over the "puddles" of your life in order to land on a dry spot so you may regroup before moving forward to seek fulfillment.

However, happiness and success are not finite destinations; rather, they are attitudes you hold as you travel along the road of life and ones that you can develop within your security career. The action of always seeking happiness and success indicates that you never feel happy or satisfied with your success because you're always in pursuit of the next thing that will make you feel that way. It is important to recognise, pause and relish the small moments of joy you encounter along your way. That is where you will find your true happiness and career success.

Author Bio and Contact Information

Jordan Wylie is a 30-year-old former soldier who was born in Blackpool, Lancashire. After joining the Army at 17, he served around the world on various training exercises and operationally in Northern Ireland and Iraq.

Since leaving the Army in 2009, he has gone on to specialise in Maritime Security and has completed over 100 High Risk missions off the coast of east and west Africa as a counter piracy specialist. He has spent two years as a Maritime Security Operations Manager and has provided consultancy services for some of the world's biggest shipping companies.

He is an experienced training instructor and manager. He has had the honour of training former military, police and government personnel from around the world and has also consulted for the International Maritime Organisation.

Jordan is a qualified and experienced lead auditor for quality management and security management systems and is one of the few consultants at present within the UK that has experience of auditing Private Maritime Security Companies against ISO PAS 28007:2012.

At present Jordan is currently the Director of Operations of a leading international security training company, The-Training-Wing. His passion is sharing his knowledge and experience with others in order to ensure other service leavers looking to pursue a career in the private security industry are well equipped for the challenges faced outside the wire.

Jordan enjoys networking and meeting new people from all different cultures and backgrounds, and he is a passionate football fan and follower of Blackpool FC.

Printed in Great Britain
by Amazon